PENS
and
NEEDLES

PENS
and
NEEDLES

Literary Caricatures by

DAVID LEVINE

LIVERIGHT  NEW YORK

1.987654321

ISBN: 0-87140-089-8

Liveright Paperbound Edition 1973

Manufactured in the United States of America

The New World

BENJAMIN FRANKLIN

RALPH WALDO EMERSON

EDGAR ALLAN POE

NATHANIEL HAWTHORNE

MARK TWAIN

STEPHEN CRANE

HENRY JAMES

THOMAS WOLFE

GERTRUDE STEIN

WILLIAM FAULKNER

F. Scott Fitzgerald

ERNEST HEMINGWAY

HENRY MILLER

T. S. ELIOT

ROBERT FROST

EDMUND WILSON

LIONEL TRILLING

ROBERT LOWELL

NORMAN MAILER

Edward Albee

SAUL BELLOW

VLADIMIR NABOKOV

JAMES BALDWIN

LeRoi Jones

JOHN UPDIKE

Philip Roth

The Continent

CATULLUS

CASANOVA

JEAN BAPTISTE RACINE

VOLTAIRE

JEAN JACQUES ROUSSEAU

HONORÉ DE BALZAC

ALEXANDER PUSHKIN

LEO TOLSTOY

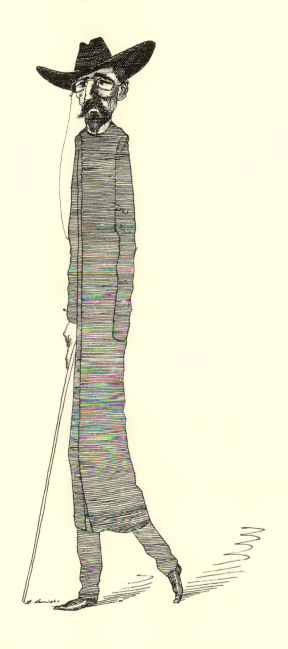

ANTON CHEKHOV

FYODOR DOSTOEVSKY

KARL MARX *(with Georg Wilhelm Friedrich Hegel)*

HENRIK IBSEN

GUSTAVE FLAUBERT

ARTHUR RIMBAUD

CHARLES BAUDELAIRE

Marcel Proust

JEAN-PAUL SARTRE

ANDRÉ GIDE

ANDRÉ MALRAUX

COLETTE

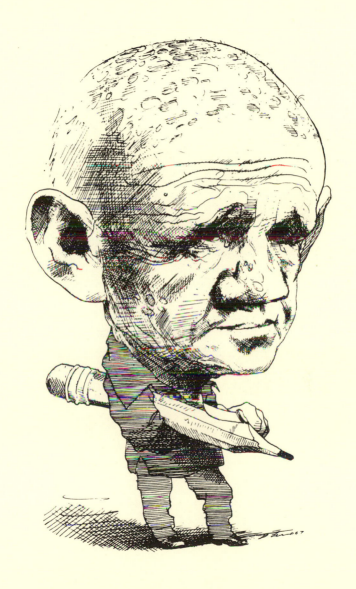

JEAN GENET

LOUIS-FERDINAND CÉLINE

SAMUEL BECKETT

ALBERTO MORAVIA

ITALO SVEVO

SIGMUND FREUD

RAINER MARIA RILKE

FRANZ KAFKA

GÜNTER GRASS

Ludwig Wittgenstein

ISAK DINESEN

S. Y. Agnon

ISAAC BABEL

VLADIMIR MAYAKOVSKY

MAXIM GORKY

MIKHAIL SHOLOKHOV

BORIS PASTERNAK

ANDREI VOZNESENSKY

YEVGENY YEVTUSHENKO

Andrei Sinyavsky

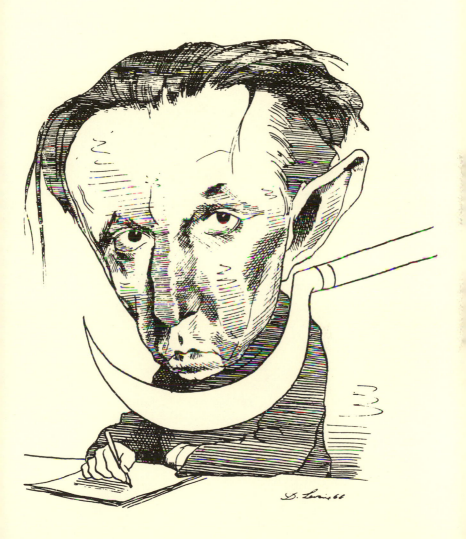

ALEXANDER SOLZHENITSYN

The British

WILLIAM SHAKESPEARE

FRANCIS BACON

JOHN MILTON

JONATHAN SWIFT

ALEXANDER POPE

EDWARD GIBBON

WILLIAM WORDSWORTH

WILLIAM BLAKE

SAMUEL TAYLOR COLERIDGE

LORD BYRON

JOHN KEATS

PERCY BYSSHE SHELLEY

ROBERT BROWNING

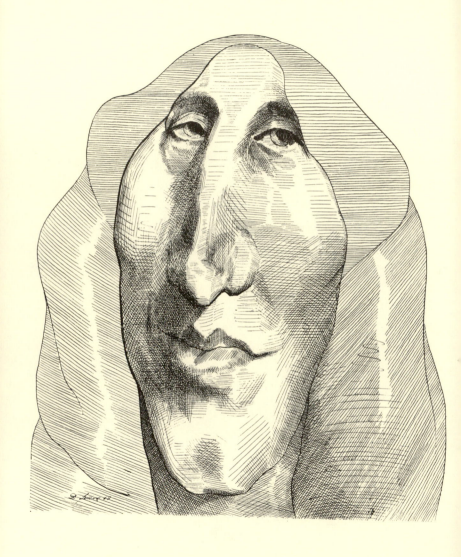

GEORGE ELIOT

CHARLES DICKENS

THOMAS CARLYLE

Cardinal John Henry Newman

More blue, that's it
Turner, now a touch of
Naples
that's
it a
drop
of water
now
blot
it,
try
scratching
on the left.
Clumsy
can't you
leave the
paper
here and
there? Did
you ever
think of
going to
Venice?

D. Levi 1864

JOHN RUSKIN

LEWIS CARROLL

BEATRIX POTTER

RUDYARD KIPLING

THOMAS HARDY

AUBREY BEARDSLEY

OSCAR WILDE

GEORGE BERNARD SHAW

Max Beerbohm

FORD MADOX FORD

ARNOLD BENNETT

E. M. FORSTER

H. G. WELLS

SIDNEY AND BEATRICE WEBB

BERTRAND RUSSELL

WILLIAM BUTLER YEATS

W. B. YEATS, D. H. LAWRENCE, WYNDHAM LEWIS,

T. S. ELIOT, EZRA POUND

LYTTON STRACHEY

LEONARD WOOLF

VIRGINIA WOOLF

JAMES JOYCE

D. H. LAWRENCE

WINSTON CHURCHILL

J. R. R. TOLKIEN

ARNOLD TOYNBEE

GRAHAM GREENE

Dame Edith Sitwell

LAWRENCE DURRELL

ANTHONY POWELL

DYLAN THOMAS

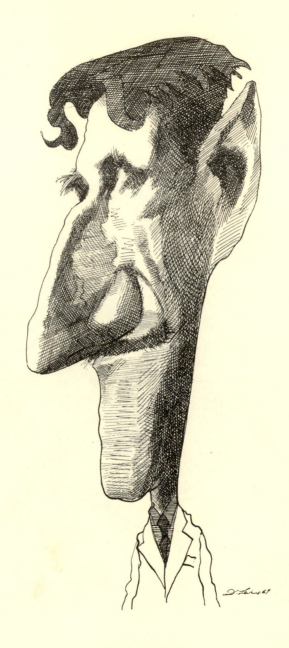

GEORGE ORWELL